How to Read Graphs

BY RACHEL HAMBY

The Child's World®
childsworld.com

Published by The Child's World®
1980 Lookout Drive • Mankato, MN 56003-1705
800-599-READ • www.childsworld.com

Photographs ©: Aleksandr Bryliaev/Shutterstock Images, cover (foreground); Shutterstock Images, cover (background), 3, 8, 9, 12, 13, 16, 17, 19, 23; iStockphoto, 5; Red Line Editorial, 7, 15, 18; Israel Mckee/Shutterstock Images, 11

ISBN 9781503823310
LCCN 2017944895

Printed in the United States of America
PA02360

ABOUT THE AUTHOR

Rachel Hamby lives in Spokane, Washington. She works for her local school district and writes fiction, nonfiction, and poetry for kids.

Table of Contents

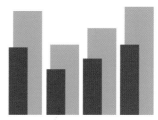

What Is a Graph?

Katie sees a new poster in the school lunchroom. It has a bar graph. Katie reads the title: "Favorite School Lunches." She looks at the graph's labels. She looks at the height of the bars. These **features** give her information. They help her make a **conclusion**.

Katie is surprised. Pizza is the most-liked lunch at her school. Katie voted for chicken. But more students chose pizza. Chicken is the third-most-liked lunch at her school.

A bar graph is just one type of graph. There are many kinds of graphs. They each show information in a different way.

Graphs can measure things such as favorite school lunches.

A graph is a picture of **data**. The data give information about a topic. A graph shows how one thing relates to another or how something changes over time. Graphs help people compare facts or find patterns. Graphs can also be used to **predict** what might happen next.

Tools for Reading Graphs

Many graphs have labels. Labels show **variables**. Some graphs have lines with labels. Each labeled line is called an axis. The x-axis is a **horizontal** line. This axis shows fixed categories that won't change. One example is the types of food students could vote for in the "Favorite School Lunches" graph. The y-axis is a **vertical** line. This axis shows the data that changed over time or across the categories or groups. In the "Favorite School Lunches" graph, the number of students was shown on the y-axis. The students were responding to the categories on the x-axis.

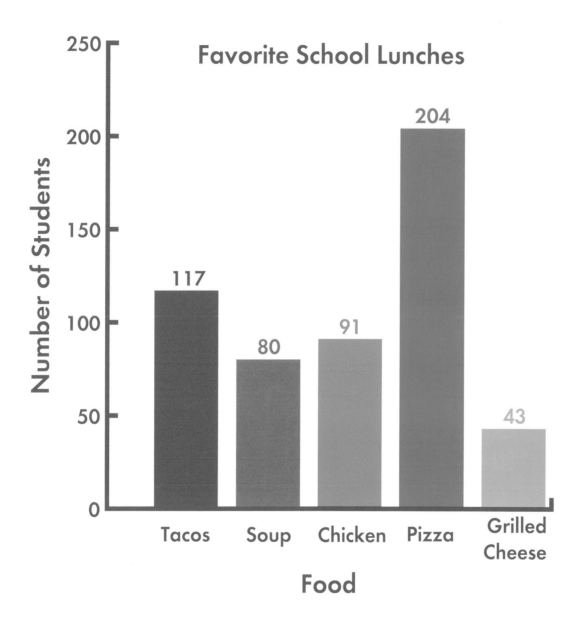

Favorite School Lunches

Number of Students

250

200 — 204

150

117

100 — 91

80

50 — 43

0

Tacos   Soup   Chicken   Pizza   Grilled Cheese

Food

The markings along an axis are the scale. Scales start where the x-axis and y-axis meet. Numbers increase as you move right along the x-axis. On the y-axis, numbers increase as you move up. The distance between two markings might equal one unit. Or it could equal five units. The scale will tell you.

Knowing about features such as scales can help you make your own graphs.

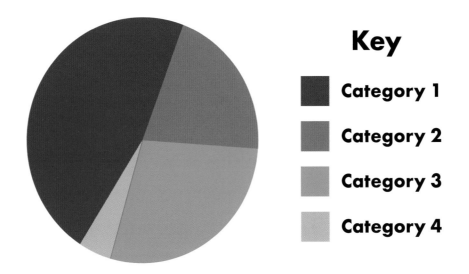

Key

■ **Category 1**

■ **Category 2**

■ **Category 3**

■ **Category 4**

Categories may be separated by color in a graph.

Graphs that use colors or **symbols** have a key. The key tells the reader what these items **represent**. Colors often represent data groups. The colors separate the different items. Each section in a pie graph is usually a different color. Each bar in a bar graph might be a different color.

Pictographs and Pie Graphs

A pictograph uses symbols to show data. Categories are labeled along one axis. Pictographs have keys. The key explains what the symbols represent. For example, a pictograph might show favorite ice cream flavors. The symbols may look like ice cream cones. The categories might include vanilla or chocolate. The key might tell you that one ice cream cone stands for two people. You count the number of ice cream cones in each category. You multiply the numbers by two. The category with the most symbols is the most popular flavor.

FAVORITE ICE CREAM FLAVORS

chocolate	
vanilla	
strawberry	

 = 2 people

Pie graphs are another kind of graph. Pie graphs are also called circle graphs. A pie graph uses a circle to show data. The sections of data look like slices of pie. Each slice is a different color. The pie graph might have a key to explain the colors.

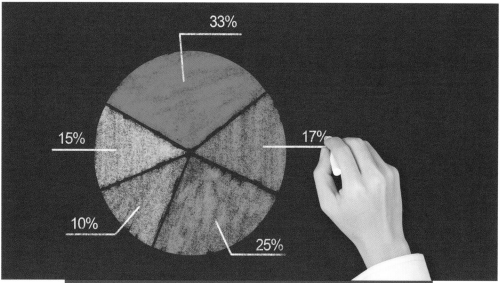

Pie graphs help people compare things as percentages.

Pie graphs help you compare the parts of a whole. They measure things as percentages. All the sections together add up to 100 percent. Larger slices stand for larger percentages. For example, a pie graph might show favorite kinds of pets. Categories might include cats and dogs. One color stands for cats. Another color stands for dogs. Each category takes up a part of the circle. The slice that stands for dogs might be bigger. This would mean that more people like dogs than cats.

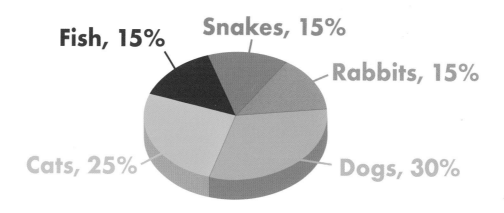

Line Plots and Line Graphs

Line plots use dots or points to show data. Line plots group data and show which groups are the most and least common. Line plots have an x-axis called a number line. They do not have a y-axis. Categories are labeled along the number line. The number line usually includes a scale. Numbers increase from left to right.

Line plots are often used for data that includes measurements. For example, a line plot may compare the number of books read by students in a class. The numbers along the number line show the number of books read.

Each student is represented by a point or a dot. The dot is placed above the matching measurement. If a student read five books, then a dot will be placed above that point on the number line. The measurement with the greatest number of dots is the most common number of books read.

Number of Books Read

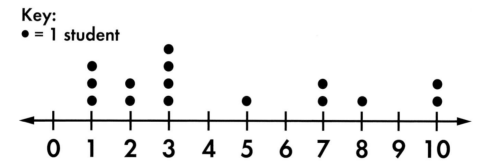

Line plots use dots to show data.

Another kind of graph is a line graph. Line graphs use dots and lines to show data. Line graphs show how something changes over time. They can also show how variables relate to one another. A line graph has an x-axis and a y-axis. Variables are labeled on each axis. The x-axis usually includes numbers and scales. For example, a line graph might measure the temperature in an area over time. Months might be labeled on the x-axis. Temperature would be labeled on the y-axis.

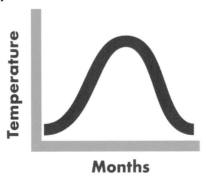

Line graphs show how things change over time.

Similar to line plots, dots are placed over each category in a line graph. First, you find the category on the x-axis. Then, you find where the dot is above that category. The dot will be level with one of the measurements on the y-axis. In the temperature line graph example, that measurement might be the highest temperature during that month.

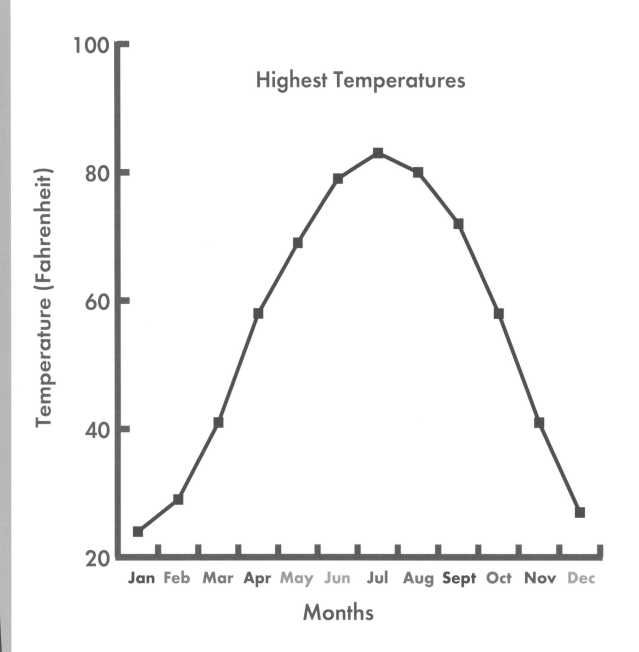

Dots on line graphs are connected by a line. The line shows how things changed over time. If a line slants up, this means that something increased. If a line slants down, this means that something decreased. In a line graph that measures temperature, you would expect the line to slant down as you move to colder months.

All graphs help people understand data. They also help people find patterns. Now you are all set to read graphs!

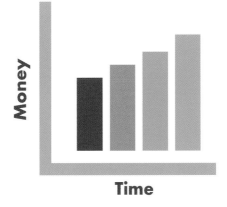

1. Which kind of graph uses percentages?
 A. a bar graph
 B. a line graph
 C. a pie graph

2. What is the purpose of a key?

3. Which kind of graph uses symbols?
   A. a pictograph
   B. a pie graph
   C. a line plot

4. What is the purpose of a line plot?

GLOSSARY

conclusion (kuhn-KLEW-zuhn) A conclusion is a decision a person makes after studying data or trends. Graphs can help people make a conclusion.

data (DAY-tuh) Data are facts or information that can be used to calculate or plan something. Graphs help people understand data.

features (FEE-churs) Features are important parts of something. Labels in graphs are features.

horizontal (hor-uh-ZON-tuhl) Horizontal means going straight across like the horizon. The x-axis on a graph is a horizontal line.

predict (pree-DIKT) To predict is to make an educated guess about what will happen. Graphs can help people predict what might happen.

represent (rep-ri-ZENT) To represent is to stand for something. Graph keys show what each symbol represents.

symbols (SIM-bulz) Symbols are shapes, letters, or pictures that stand for something else. Pictographs have symbols.

variables (VAIR-ee-uh-buhlz) Variables are things that can change over time. All graphs use variables.

vertical (VUR-tuh-kuhl) Vertical means going up and down. The y-axis on a graph is a vertical line.

TO LEARN MORE

In the Library

Dee, Nora. *Making Circle Graphs.* New York, NY: Gareth Stevens, 2015.

Pistoia, Sara. *Graphs.* Mankato, MN: The Child's World, 2014.

On the Web

Visit our Web site for links about how to read graphs:
childsworld.com/links

Note to Parents, Teachers, and Librarians: We routinely verify our Web links to make sure
they are safe and active sites. So encourage your readers to check them out!

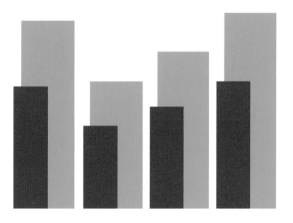

INDEX

ANSWER KEY

1. **Which kind of graph uses percentages?** C. a pie graph

2. **What is the purpose of a key?** A key explains what colors or symbols represent.

3. **Which kind of graph uses symbols?** A. a pictograph

4. **What is the purpose of a line plot?** A line plot shows which groups or categories are the most and least common.